eBook
Upload & Update Log
Indie Book Management

Book # _____

From: _____ to _____

WestWard Journals
WestWard Books
Payson, Arizona

WestWard Journals

Copyright © 2018 Marsha Ward

WestWard Books

Cover Photo by Norwood Themes at Unsplash

ISBN-13: 978-1-947306-10-3

INTRODUCTION

This Log contains space to make note of upload and update details for six self-published ebooks. The book is designed to be used with Kindle Direct Publishing. It contains ample pages for notes about updates and changes, which should help keep track of any details the Indie or Self-Publishing Author and Publisher may need.

MY PROJECT IDEAS

_____

_____

_____

_____

_____

_____

_____

_____

_____

_____

_____

_____

_____

_____

_____

_____

_____

_____

_____

_____

_____

MY BOOKS

Book 1 Title _____   Page 1
        _____
        _____

Book 2 Title _____   Page 9
        _____
        _____

Book 3 Title _____   Page 17
        _____
        _____

Book 4 Title _____   Page 25
        _____
        _____

Book 5 Title _____   Page 33
        _____
        _____

Book 6 Title _____   Page 41
        _____
        _____

MORE PROJECT IDEAS

_____

_____

_____

_____

_____

_____

_____

_____

_____

_____

_____

_____

_____

_____

_____

_____

_____

_____

_____

_____

_____

_____

BOOK 1 - Date _____

Kindle eBook Details

Language _____

Book Title _____

Subtitle _____

Series _____ # _____

Edition Number (optional) _____

Author _____

Contributors (opt) _____

_____

_____

_____

Description: _____

_____

_____

_____

_____

_____

_____

_____

_____

_____

_____

_____

_____

Publishing Rights (circle or underline one)

      I own the copyright

      This is a public domain work

Book Title _____

Keywords (seven words or phrases)

_____

_____

_____

_____

_____

_____

_____

Categories (two)

_____

_____

_____

_____

Age & Grade Range

Children's Book age range (optional)

    Minimum ____   Maximum ____

U.S. grade range

    Minimum ____   Maximum ____

Adult Content   No   Yes

Kindle eBook Content

Manuscript

    Digital Rights Management (DRM)

    Enable DRM on this Kindle eBooks?

        Yes ____   No ____

Book Title _____

Recommended formats for Kindle eBooks:

.doc, .docx, HTML, MOBI, ePub, RTF, Plain Text, and KPF.

Upload eBook manuscript

File name _____

Uploaded   Date _____

Spell Check

    ("Ignore All" doesn't always work)

File Updated   Date _____

File Updated   Date _____

File Updated   Date _____

Interior Formatter _____

Contact Info: _____

Cost: _____

Kindle eBook Cover (check one)

    ___ Use Cover Creator to make your book cover

    ___ Upload a cover you already have (JPG/TIFF only)

Upload your cover file

File name _____

Uploaded   Date _____

Kindle eBook Preview via Online Previewer

    ___ Launch Previewer   Approved date: _____

Downloadable Preview Options

    ___ On your computer   ___ On your Kindle device

Book Title _____

      Cover Updated   Date _____

      Cover Updated   Date _____

      Cover Updated   Date _____

      Cover Designer _____

      Contact Info: _____

      Cost: _____

ISBN (Optional Choice)

      Kindle ISBN _____

      Your ISBN _____

      Publisher (optional) _____

Kindle eBook Pricing

KDP Select Enrollment (Optional)   Yes ___   No ___

Territories (check one)

      ___ All territories

      ___ Individual territories (Note all your choices below)

_____

_____

_____

_____

_____

_____

_____

_____

Book Title _____

Royalty & Pricing - Select a royalty plan and set your Kindle eBook list prices below.

_____ 30%   _____ 70%

Your book file size after conversion is _____

Primary Marketplace _____

List Price Chosen _____   Currency _____

Rate _____   Delivery _____   Royalty _____

* Other Marketplace _____

List Price Chosen _____   Currency _____

Rate _____   Delivery _____   Royalty _____

* Other Marketplace _____

List Price Chosen _____   Currency _____

Rate _____   Delivery _____   Royalty _____

* Other Marketplace _____

List Price Chosen _____   Currency _____

Rate _____   Delivery _____   Royalty _____

* Other Marketplace _____

List Price Chosen _____   Currency _____

Rate _____   Delivery _____   Royalty _____

* Other Marketplace _____

List Price Chosen _____   Currency _____

Rate _____   Delivery _____   Royalty _____

Book Title _____

* Other Marketplace _____

List Price Chosen _____ Currency _____

Rate _____ Delivery _____ Royalty _____

* Other Marketplace _____

List Price Chosen _____ Currency _____

Rate _____ Delivery _____ Royalty _____

* Other Marketplace _____

List Price Chosen _____ Currency _____

Rate _____ Delivery _____ Royalty _____

* Other Marketplace _____

List Price Chosen _____ Currency _____

Rate _____ Delivery _____ Royalty _____

* Other Marketplace _____

List Price Chosen _____ Currency _____

Rate _____ Delivery _____ Royalty _____

* Other Marketplace _____

List Price Chosen _____ Currency _____

Rate _____ Delivery _____ Royalty _____

* Other Marketplace _____

List Price Chosen _____ Currency _____

Rate _____ Delivery _____ Royalty _____

Book Title _____

Matchbook

    ___ Enroll my book in Kindle Matchbook

Book Lending

    ___ Allow Kindle Book Lending

Terms & Conditions ___ Read

    Save as Draft Date _____

    Clicked Publish Your Kindle eBook Date _____

    Published Notice from KDP Date _____

Note Date & Changes Made

_____

_____

_____

_____

_____

_____

_____

_____

_____

_____

_____

_____

_____

_____

_____

_____

Book Title _____

Note Date & Changes Made

_____

_____

_____

_____

_____

_____

_____

_____

_____

_____

_____

_____

_____

_____

_____

_____

_____

_____

_____

_____

_____

_____

_____

_____

_____

BOOK 2 - Date _____

Kindle eBook Details

Language _____

Book Title _____

Subtitle _____

Series _____ # _____

Edition Number (optional) _____

Author _____

Contributors (opt) _____

_____

_____

_____

Description: _____

_____

_____

_____

_____

_____

_____

_____

_____

_____

_____

_____

Publishing Rights (circle or underline one)

I own the copyright

This is a public domain work

Book Title _____

    Keywords (seven words or phrases)

    _____

    _____

    _____

    _____

    _____

    _____

    _____

    Categories (two)

    _____

    _____

    _____

    Age & Grade Range

    Children's Book age range (optional)

        Minimum ____   Maximum ____

    U.S. grade range

        Minimum ____   Maximum ____

    Adult Content   No   Yes

Kindle eBook Content

Manuscript

    Digital Rights Management (DRM)

    Enable DRM on this Kindle eBooks?

        Yes ____   No ____

Book Title _____

Recommended formats for Kindle eBooks:

.doc, .docx, HTML, MOBI, ePub, RTF, Plain Text, and KPF.

Upload eBook manuscript

File name _____

Uploaded   Date _____

Spell Check

　　　("Ignore All" doesn't always work)

File Updated   Date _____

File Updated   Date _____

File Updated   Date _____

Interior Formatter _____

Contact Info: _____

Cost: _____

Kindle eBook Cover (check one)

　　___ Use Cover Creator to make your book cover

　　___ Upload a cover you already have (JPG/TIFF only)

Upload your cover file

File name _____

Uploaded   Date _____

Kindle eBook Preview via Online Previewer

　　___ Launch Previewer   Approved date: _____

Downloadable Preview Options

　　___ On your computer   ___ On your Kindle device

Book Title _____

    Cover Updated   Date _____

    Cover Updated   Date _____

    Cover Updated   Date _____

    Cover Designer _____

    Contact Info: _____

    Cost: _____

ISBN (Optional Choice)

    Kindle ISBN _____

    Your ISBN _____

    Publisher (optional) _____

Kindle eBook Pricing

KDP Select Enrollment (Optional)   Yes ___   No ___

Territories (check one)

    ___ All territories

    ___ Individual territories (Note all your choices below)

_____

_____

_____

_____

_____

_____

_____

_____

_____

Book Title _____

Royalty & Pricing - Select a royalty plan and set your Kindle eBook list prices below.

____ 30%   ____ 70%

Your book file size after conversion is _____

Primary Marketplace _____

List Price Chosen _____   Currency _____

Rate _____   Delivery _____   Royalty _____

* Other Marketplace _____

List Price Chosen _____   Currency _____

Rate _____   Delivery _____   Royalty _____

* Other Marketplace _____

List Price Chosen _____   Currency _____

Rate _____   Delivery _____   Royalty _____

* Other Marketplace _____

List Price Chosen _____   Currency _____

Rate _____   Delivery _____   Royalty _____

* Other Marketplace _____

List Price Chosen _____   Currency _____

Rate _____   Delivery _____   Royalty _____

* Other Marketplace _____

List Price Chosen _____   Currency _____

Rate _____   Delivery _____   Royalty _____

Book Title _____

* Other Marketplace _____

List Price Chosen _____   Currency _____

Rate _____   Delivery _____   Royalty _____

* Other Marketplace _____

List Price Chosen _____   Currency _____

Rate _____   Delivery _____   Royalty _____

* Other Marketplace _____

List Price Chosen _____   Currency _____

Rate _____   Delivery _____   Royalty _____

* Other Marketplace _____

List Price Chosen _____   Currency _____

Rate _____   Delivery _____   Royalty _____

* Other Marketplace _____

List Price Chosen _____   Currency _____

Rate _____   Delivery _____   Royalty _____

* Other Marketplace _____

List Price Chosen _____   Currency _____

Rate _____   Delivery _____   Royalty _____

* Other Marketplace _____

List Price Chosen _____   Currency _____

Rate _____   Delivery _____   Royalty _____

Book Title _____

Matchbook

____ Enroll my book in Kindle Matchbook

Book Lending

____ Allow Kindle Book Lending

Terms & Conditions ____ Read

Save as Draft Date _____

Clicked Publish Your Kindle eBook Date _____

Published Notice from KDP Date _____

Note Date & Changes Made

_____

_____

_____

_____

_____

_____

_____

_____

_____

_____

_____

_____

_____

_____

Book Title _____

Note Date & Changes Made

_____
_____
_____
_____
_____
_____
_____
_____
_____
_____
_____
_____
_____
_____
_____
_____
_____
_____
_____
_____
_____
_____
_____
_____

BOOK 3 - Date _____

Kindle eBook Details

Language _____

Book Title _____

Subtitle _____

Series _____ # ____

Edition Number (optional) _____

Author _____

Contributors (opt) _____

_____

_____

_____

Description: _____

_____

_____

_____

_____

_____

_____

_____

_____

_____

_____

_____

Publishing Rights (circle or underline one)

I own the copyright

This is a public domain work

17

Book Title _____

    Keywords (seven words or phrases)

    _____

    _____

    _____

    _____

    _____

    _____

    _____

    Categories (two)

    _____

    _____

    _____

    _____

    Age & Grade Range

    Children's Book age range (optional)

        Minimum ____   Maximum ____

    U.S. grade range

        Minimum ____   Maximum ____

    Adult Content   No   Yes

Kindle eBook Content

Manuscript

    Digital Rights Management (DRM)

    Enable DRM on this Kindle eBooks?

        Yes ____   No ____

Book Title _____

Recommended formats for Kindle eBooks:

.doc, .docx, HTML, MOBI, ePub, RTF, Plain Text, and KPF.

Upload eBook manuscript

File name _____

Uploaded   Date _____

Spell Check

     ("Ignore All" doesn't always work)

File Updated   Date _____

File Updated   Date _____

File Updated   Date _____

Interior Formatter _____

Contact Info: _____

Cost: _____

Kindle eBook Cover (check one)

   ___ Use Cover Creator to make your book cover

   ___ Upload a cover you already have (JPG/TIFF only)

Upload your cover file

File name _____

Uploaded   Date _____

Kindle eBook Preview via Online Previewer

   ___ Launch Previewer   Approved date: _____

Downloadable Preview Options

   ___ On your computer   ___ On your Kindle device

Book Title _____

Cover Updated   Date _____

Cover Updated   Date _____

Cover Updated   Date _____

Cover Designer _____

Contact Info: _____

Cost: _____

ISBN (Optional Choice)

Kindle ISBN _____

Your ISBN _____

Publisher (optional) _____

Kindle eBook Pricing

KDP Select Enrollment (Optional)   Yes ____   No ____

Territories (check one)

____ All territories

____ Individual territories (Note all your choices below)

_____

_____

_____

_____

_____

_____

_____

_____

_____

_____

Book Title _____

Royalty & Pricing - Select a royalty plan and set your Kindle
eBook list prices below.

    ___ 30%   ___ 70%

Your book file size after conversion is _____

Primary Marketplace _____

List Price Chosen _____   Currency _____

Rate _____   Delivery _____   Royalty _____

* Other Marketplace _____

List Price Chosen _____   Currency _____

Rate _____   Delivery _____   Royalty _____

* Other Marketplace _____

List Price Chosen _____   Currency _____

Rate _____   Delivery _____   Royalty _____

* Other Marketplace _____

List Price Chosen _____   Currency _____

Rate _____   Delivery _____   Royalty _____

* Other Marketplace _____

List Price Chosen _____   Currency _____

Rate _____   Delivery _____   Royalty _____

* Other Marketplace _____

List Price Chosen _____   Currency _____

Rate _____   Delivery _____   Royalty _____

Book Title _____

* Other Marketplace _____
List Price Chosen _____ Currency _____
Rate _____ Delivery _____ Royalty _____

* Other Marketplace _____
List Price Chosen _____ Currency _____
Rate _____ Delivery _____ Royalty _____

* Other Marketplace _____
List Price Chosen _____ Currency _____
Rate _____ Delivery _____ Royalty _____

* Other Marketplace _____
List Price Chosen _____ Currency _____
Rate _____ Delivery _____ Royalty _____

* Other Marketplace _____
List Price Chosen _____ Currency _____
Rate _____ Delivery _____ Royalty _____

* Other Marketplace _____
List Price Chosen _____ Currency _____
Rate _____ Delivery _____ Royalty _____

* Other Marketplace _____
List Price Chosen _____ Currency _____
Rate _____ Delivery _____ Royalty _____

Book Title _____

Matchbook

_____ Enroll my book in Kindle Matchbook

Book Lending

_____ Allow Kindle Book Lending

Terms & Conditions _____ Read

Save as Draft Date _____

Clicked Publish Your Kindle eBook Date _____

Published Notice from KDP Date _____

Note Date & Changes Made

_____

_____

_____

_____

_____

_____

_____

_____

_____

_____

_____

_____

_____

_____

_____

Book Title _____

Note Date & Changes Made

_____

_____

_____

_____

_____

_____

_____

_____

_____

_____

_____

_____

_____

_____

_____

_____

_____

_____

_____

_____

_____

_____

_____

BOOK 4 - Date _____

Kindle eBook Details

Language _____

Book Title _____

Subtitle _____

Series _____ # ____

Edition Number (optional) _____

Author _____

Contributors (opt) _____

_____

_____

_____

Description: _____

_____

_____

_____

_____

_____

_____

_____

_____

_____

_____

_____

_____

Publishing Rights (circle or underline one)

       I own the copyright

       This is a public domain work

Book Title _____

Keywords (seven words or phrases)

_____

_____

_____

_____

_____

_____

_____

Categories (two)

_____

_____

_____

Age & Grade Range

Children's Book age range (optional)

    Minimum _____   Maximum _____

U.S. grade range

    Minimum _____   Maximum _____

Adult Content   No   Yes

Kindle eBook Content

Manuscript

    Digital Rights Management (DRM)

    Enable DRM on this Kindle eBooks?

        Yes _____   No _____

Book Title _____

Recommended formats for Kindle eBooks:

.doc, .docx, HTML, MOBI, ePub, RTF, Plain Text, and KPF.

Upload eBook manuscript

File name _____

Uploaded   Date _____

Spell Check

    ("Ignore All" doesn't always work)

File Updated   Date _____

File Updated   Date _____

File Updated   Date _____

Interior Formatter _____

Contact Info: _____

Cost: _____

Kindle eBook Cover (check one)

    ___ Use Cover Creator to make your book cover

    ___ Upload a cover you already have (JPG/TIFF only)

Upload your cover file

File name _____

Uploaded   Date _____

Kindle eBook Preview via Online Previewer

    ___ Launch Previewer   Approved date: _____

Downloadable Preview Options

    ___ On your computer   ___ On your Kindle device

Book Title _____

    Cover Updated   Date _____

    Cover Updated   Date _____

    Cover Updated   Date _____

    Cover Designer _____

    Contact Info: _____

    Cost: _____

ISBN (Optional Choice)

    Kindle ISBN _____

    Your ISBN _____

    Publisher (optional) _____

Kindle eBook Pricing

KDP Select Enrollment (Optional)   Yes ___   No ___

Territories (check one)

    ___ All territories

    ___ Individual territories (Note all your choices below)

_____

_____

_____

_____

_____

_____

_____

_____

_____

Book Title _____

Royalty & Pricing - Select a royalty plan and set your Kindle eBook list prices below.

___ 30%   ___ 70%

Your book file size after conversion is _____

Primary Marketplace _____

List Price Chosen _____ Currency _____

Rate _____ Delivery _____ Royalty _____

* Other Marketplace _____

List Price Chosen _____ Currency _____

Rate _____ Delivery _____ Royalty _____

* Other Marketplace _____

List Price Chosen _____ Currency _____

Rate _____ Delivery _____ Royalty _____

* Other Marketplace _____

List Price Chosen _____ Currency _____

Rate _____ Delivery _____ Royalty _____

* Other Marketplace _____

List Price Chosen _____ Currency _____

Rate _____ Delivery _____ Royalty _____

* Other Marketplace _____

List Price Chosen _____ Currency _____

Rate _____ Delivery _____ Royalty _____

Book Title _____

* Other Marketplace _____

List Price Chosen _____   Currency _____

Rate _____   Delivery _____   Royalty _____

* Other Marketplace _____

List Price Chosen _____   Currency _____

Rate _____   Delivery _____   Royalty _____

* Other Marketplace _____

List Price Chosen _____   Currency _____

Rate _____   Delivery _____   Royalty _____

* Other Marketplace _____

List Price Chosen _____   Currency _____

Rate _____   Delivery _____   Royalty _____

* Other Marketplace _____

List Price Chosen _____   Currency _____

Rate _____   Delivery _____   Royalty _____

* Other Marketplace _____

List Price Chosen _____   Currency _____

Rate _____   Delivery _____   Royalty _____

* Other Marketplace _____

List Price Chosen _____   Currency _____

Rate _____   Delivery _____   Royalty _____

Book Title _____

Matchbook

_____ Enroll my book in Kindle Matchbook

Book Lending

_____ Allow Kindle Book Lending

Terms & Conditions _____ Read

Save as Draft Date _____

Clicked Publish Your Kindle eBook Date _____

Published Notice from KDP Date _____

Note Date & Changes Made

_____

_____

_____

_____

_____

_____

_____

_____

_____

_____

_____

_____

_____

_____

Book Title _____

Note Date & Changes Made

_____
_____
_____
_____
_____
_____
_____
_____
_____
_____
_____
_____
_____
_____
_____
_____
_____
_____
_____
_____
_____
_____
_____
_____
_____

BOOK 5 - Date _____

Kindle eBook Details

Language _____

Book Title _____

Subtitle _____

Series _____ # ____

Edition Number (optional) _____

Author _____

Contributors (opt) _____

_____

_____

_____

Description: _____

_____

_____

_____

_____

_____

_____

_____

_____

_____

_____

_____

_____

Publishing Rights (circle or underline one)

I own the copyright

This is a public domain work

Book Title _____

Keywords (seven words or phrases)

_____

_____

_____

_____

_____

_____

_____

Categories (two)

_____

_____

_____

Age & Grade Range

Children's Book age range (optional)

    Minimum ____   Maximum ____

U.S. grade range

    Minimum ____   Maximum ____

Adult Content   No   Yes

Kindle eBook Content

Manuscript

    Digital Rights Management (DRM)

    Enable DRM on this Kindle eBooks?

        Yes ____   No ____

Book Title _____

Recommended formats for Kindle eBooks:

.doc, .docx, HTML, MOBI, ePub, RTF, Plain Text, and KPF.

Upload eBook manuscript

File name _____

Uploaded   Date _____

Spell Check

    ("Ignore All" doesn't always work)

File Updated   Date _____

File Updated   Date _____

File Updated   Date _____

Interior Formatter _____

Contact Info: _____

Cost: _____

Kindle eBook Cover (check one)

    ___ Use Cover Creator to make your book cover

    ___ Upload a cover you already have (JPG/TIFF only)

Upload your cover file

File name _____

Uploaded   Date _____

Kindle eBook Preview via Online Previewer

    ___ Launch Previewer   Approved date: _____

Downloadable Preview Options

    ___ On your computer   ___ On your Kindle device

Book Title _____

    Cover Updated   Date _____

    Cover Updated   Date _____

    Cover Updated   Date _____

    Cover Designer _____

    Contact Info: _____

    Cost: _____

ISBN (Optional Choice)

    Kindle ISBN _____

    Your ISBN _____

    Publisher (optional) _____

Kindle eBook Pricing

KDP Select Enrollment (Optional)   Yes ____   No ____

Territories (check one)

    ____ All territories

    ____ Individual territories (Note all your choices below)

_____

_____

_____

_____

_____

_____

_____

_____

_____

Book Title _____

Royalty & Pricing - Select a royalty plan and set your Kindle
eBook list prices below.

____ 30%   ____ 70%

Your book file size after conversion is _____

Primary Marketplace _____

List Price Chosen _____   Currency _____

Rate _____   Delivery _____   Royalty _____

* Other Marketplace _____

List Price Chosen _____   Currency _____

Rate _____   Delivery _____   Royalty _____

* Other Marketplace _____

List Price Chosen _____   Currency _____

Rate _____   Delivery _____   Royalty _____

* Other Marketplace _____

List Price Chosen _____   Currency _____

Rate _____   Delivery _____   Royalty _____

* Other Marketplace _____

List Price Chosen _____   Currency _____

Rate _____   Delivery _____   Royalty _____

* Other Marketplace _____

List Price Chosen _____   Currency _____

Rate _____   Delivery _____   Royalty _____

Book Title _____

* Other Marketplace _____

List Price Chosen _____ Currency _____

Rate _____ Delivery _____ Royalty _____

* Other Marketplace _____

List Price Chosen _____ Currency _____

Rate _____ Delivery _____ Royalty _____

* Other Marketplace _____

List Price Chosen _____ Currency _____

Rate _____ Delivery _____ Royalty _____

* Other Marketplace _____

List Price Chosen _____ Currency _____

Rate _____ Delivery _____ Royalty _____

* Other Marketplace _____

List Price Chosen _____ Currency _____

Rate _____ Delivery _____ Royalty _____

* Other Marketplace _____

List Price Chosen _____ Currency _____

Rate _____ Delivery _____ Royalty _____

* Other Marketplace _____

List Price Chosen _____ Currency _____

Rate _____ Delivery _____ Royalty _____

Book Title _____

Matchbook

____ Enroll my book in Kindle Matchbook

Book Lending

____ Allow Kindle Book Lending

Terms & Conditions ____ Read

Save as Draft Date _____

Clicked Publish Your Kindle eBook Date _____

Published Notice from KDP Date _____

Note Date & Changes Made

_____

_____

_____

_____

_____

_____

_____

_____

_____

_____

_____

_____

_____

_____

_____

_____

Book Title _____

Note Date & Changes Made

_____

_____

_____

_____

_____

_____

_____

_____

_____

_____

_____

_____

_____

_____

_____

_____

_____

_____

_____

_____

_____

_____

_____

BOOK 6 - Date _____

Kindle eBook Details

Language _____

Book Title _____

Subtitle _____

Series _____ # ____

Edition Number (optional) _____

Author _____

Contributors (opt) _____

_____

_____

_____

Description: _____

_____

_____

_____

_____

_____

_____

_____

_____

_____

_____

_____

_____

Publishing Rights (circle or underline one)

I own the copyright

This is a public domain work

Book Title _____

Keywords (seven words or phrases)

_____

_____

_____

_____

_____

_____

_____

Categories (two)

_____

_____

_____

_____

Age & Grade Range

Children's Book age range (optional)

    Minimum ____   Maximum ____

U.S. grade range

    Minimum ____   Maximum ____

Adult Content   No   Yes

Kindle eBook Content

Manuscript

    Digital Rights Management (DRM)

    Enable DRM on this Kindle eBooks?

        Yes ____   No ____

Book Title _____

Recommended formats for Kindle eBooks:

.doc, .docx, HTML, MOBI, ePub, RTF, Plain Text, and KPF.

Upload eBook manuscript

File name _____

Uploaded   Date _____

Spell Check

    ("Ignore All" doesn't always work)

File Updated   Date _____

File Updated   Date _____

File Updated   Date _____

Interior Formatter _____

Contact Info: _____

Cost: _____

Kindle eBook Cover (check one)

    ___ Use Cover Creator to make your book cover

    ___ Upload a cover you already have (JPG/TIFF only)

Upload your cover file

File name _____

Uploaded   Date _____

Kindle eBook Preview via Online Previewer

    ___ Launch Previewer   Approved date: _____

Downloadable Preview Options

    ___ On your computer   ___ On your Kindle device

Book Title _____

    Cover Updated   Date _____

    Cover Updated   Date _____

    Cover Updated   Date _____

    Cover Designer _____

    Contact Info: _____

    Cost: _____

ISBN (Optional Choice)

    Kindle ISBN _____

    Your ISBN _____

    Publisher (optional) _____

Kindle eBook Pricing

KDP Select Enrollment (Optional)   Yes ____   No ____

Territories (check one)

    ____ All territories

    ____ Individual territories (Note all your choices below)

_____

_____

_____

_____

_____

_____

_____

_____

Book Title _____

Royalty & Pricing - Select a royalty plan and set your Kindle eBook list prices below.

_____ 30%   _____ 70%

Your book file size after conversion is _____

Primary Marketplace _____

List Price Chosen _____   Currency _____

Rate _____   Delivery _____   Royalty _____

* Other Marketplace _____

List Price Chosen _____   Currency _____

Rate _____   Delivery _____   Royalty _____

* Other Marketplace _____

List Price Chosen _____   Currency _____

Rate _____   Delivery _____   Royalty _____

* Other Marketplace _____

List Price Chosen _____   Currency _____

Rate _____   Delivery _____   Royalty _____

* Other Marketplace _____

List Price Chosen _____   Currency _____

Rate _____   Delivery _____   Royalty _____

* Other Marketplace _____

List Price Chosen _____   Currency _____

Rate _____   Delivery _____   Royalty _____

Book Title _____

* Other Marketplace _____

List Price Chosen _____   Currency _____

Rate _____   Delivery _____   Royalty _____

* Other Marketplace _____

List Price Chosen _____   Currency _____

Rate _____   Delivery _____   Royalty _____

* Other Marketplace _____

List Price Chosen _____   Currency _____

Rate _____   Delivery _____   Royalty _____

* Other Marketplace _____

List Price Chosen _____   Currency _____

Rate _____   Delivery _____   Royalty _____

* Other Marketplace _____

List Price Chosen _____   Currency _____

Rate _____   Delivery _____   Royalty _____

* Other Marketplace _____

List Price Chosen _____   Currency _____

Rate _____   Delivery _____   Royalty _____

* Other Marketplace _____

List Price Chosen _____   Currency _____

Rate _____   Delivery _____   Royalty _____

Book Title _____

Matchbook

    ___ Enroll my book in Kindle Matchbook

Book Lending

    ___ Allow Kindle Book Lending

Terms & Conditions ___ Read

    Save as Draft Date _____

    Clicked Publish Your Kindle eBook Date _____

    Published Notice from KDP Date _____

Note Date & Changes Made

_____

_____

_____

_____

_____

_____

_____

_____

_____

_____

_____

_____

_____

_____

_____

Book Title _____

Note Date & Changes Made

_____

_____

_____

_____

_____

_____

_____

_____

_____

_____

_____

_____

_____

_____

_____

_____

_____

_____

_____

_____

_____

_____

_____

_____

_____

_____

_____

About the Creator of WestWard Journals

Marsha Ward writes authentic historical fiction, and nonfiction having to do with writing. Her novels include The Owen Family Saga series, the Shenandoah Neighbors series, and many other works of fiction. Her nonfiction books include *The Checklist: Indie Publishing My Way, Rapid Recipes for Writers . . . And Other Busy People,* and *From Julia's Kitchen: Owen Family Cookery.*

Find her online at Amazon or at marshaward.com.